The People's H

Out of Darkness
Came Light

by

Derek Gillum

Derek Gillum

CHILTON COLLIERY

Chilton Colliery. The first sinking of a pit on this site in the 1830s was a failure before the colliery above was sunk in 1872 by H. Stobart & Co. The pit closed in 1966.

Copyright Derek Gillum 2005

First published in 2005 by

The People's History Ltd
Suite 1, Byron House
Seaham Grange Business Park, Seaham
County Durham SR7 0PY

ISBN: 1 902527 57 7

Contents

Acknowledgements   4

Introduction   5

1.   The Durham Coalfield   7

2.   Men at Work   31

3.   Colliery Communities   45

4.   The Durham Miners' Gala   59

5.   Pit Banners   89

6.   Preserving Our Heritage   115

Acknowledgements

I would like to thank the following for their help in the compiling of this book:

Arthur Pike, George Rowe & Pat Simmons (Houghton & Lambton Banner Group), Tony Westgarth, Andrew Clark, Bill Middleton (Thornley Banner Group), Jean Gillum, Dave Hopper (NUM Durham Area), Arthur Youern, Tom Arkley (Chairman, Silksworth & District Banner Group), John Cairns (Wingate Banner Group), Eddie Carmody, Terry Bannister, Ted Laskey, Chris Sargent, Mr & Mrs T. Potts, John & Jack Gleghorn, Ron Gray, Bas Richardson, Silksworth Mining Society, Peter Frecker (photographs of Wearmouth underground), Mr O. McGuire, Mr & Mrs H. Brown, Shaun Ryan, Paul Watson and David Gillum.

I dedicate this book to my father, Fred Gillum.

My dad worked at Ryhope Colliery from the age of 15 and worked there until 1960. After a dispute at Second West Ryhope Colliery, he started work at Seaham Colliery and stayed there until his death in 1970, when he was fifty years old. My father worked thirty-five years in the mining industry.

The book is also dedicated to all those other men who worked and died in the Durham Coalfield.

Lest We Forget.

Two marras – Jack Burlinson and Derek Gillum – outside the pit offices at Vane Tempest Colliery in 1986.

Introduction

Out of Darkness Came Light, a very fitting title for a book on the mining industry in the once mighty Durham Coalfield.

The period it covers is from the inception of the Durham Miners' Association in 1869 to the present day, a whole history of the struggles and achievements of the Union, its members, their families and communities. Obviously no book could hope to cover all of the relevant history of this period, but this is an attempt by a former coalminer to portray how he has analysed the history and incorporated the events and times that he lived through and experienced.

It relates to the individuals and characters that were numerous in the coalfields, the stories and tales of mines and miners, the collieries and the communities that passed through a period of tremendous conflict between capital and labour, two world wars and the miners' dream, the nationalisation of the coal industry.

Since 1993, and the closure of the last deep mine in the former Durham Coalfield, an event that seemed unthinkable not so long ago, there has been a resurgence in the Durham Miners' Gala, an event that commenced in 1871. Perhaps this epitomises the spirit and determination of the people and their communities not to let coalmining die.

There is certainly a rich seam of history from a unique industry, the story of which needs to be told.

Dave Hopper, General Secretary,
National Union of Mineworkers Durham Area

Dave Hopper with the Washington Glebe Lodge Banner. One side has the inscription 'Unity is Strength' while the other side has a portrait of the Labour Party politician, Nye Bevan. The union is still active despite there being no collieries in the county. Dave Hopper, alongside, Dave Guy (President), help to co-ordinate a series of programmes to support former mineworkers and their families.

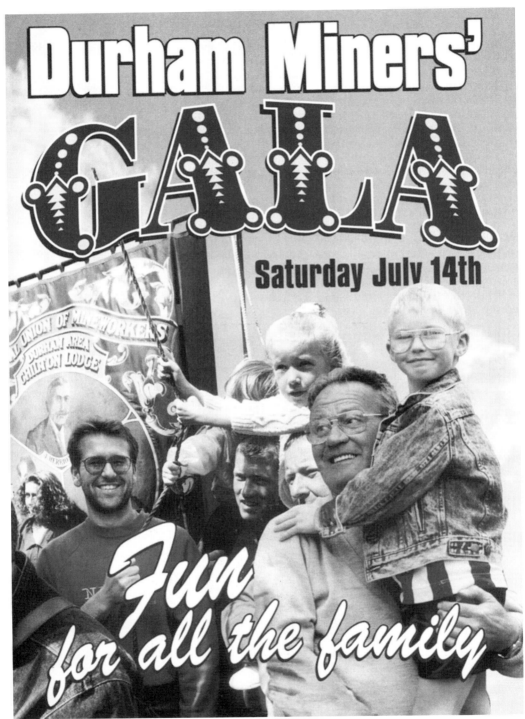

An advert for the Durham Miners' Gala – The Big Meeting.

THE DURHAM COALFIELD

Easington Colliery. Sinking was completed in 1910. The colliery had three shafts and closed in November 1993.

Easington Colliery, after closure, showing the pit baths on the left.

Vane Tempest Colliery showing the Vane shaft on the right and the Tempest shaft on the left. The sinking of this Seaham pit began in December 1923. The sinking of the Tempest shaft was completed on 12th January 1928, to the depth of 2,116 feet. The Vane shaft was completed on 18th June 1928, to the depth of 1,893 feet. The shafts were 200 feet apart and each had a diameter of 21 feet.

The Maudlin Seam at the colliery was closed around 1982. A roadway was driven from the Maudlin Seam out to the North Sea but this was never worked due to the coal running too near to the sea bed. The future of the Vane was seriously affected by the offshore fault. In the early 1980s the pit was combined with Seaham Colliery.

Ten years later, Vane Tempest was included in British Coal's closure plan of 31 pits. The colliery was closed on 4th June 1993. It was a sad loss to the Durham Coalfield as the Vane was a happly place to work.

Right: Dismantling old crawlers at Vane Tempest during reconstruction in 1958.

Shaft reconstruction at Vane Tempest Colliery in 1958 – moving a skip into the Tempest air lock. Left to right: W. Brunning (blacksmith), P. Lenox (welder), D. O'Connor (blacksmith's striker), T. Pawsy (shaftman), unknown, unknown, J. Atkinson (blacksmith) and Bert Dobson (labourer).

More reconstruction at the Vane shaft bottom in 1958 when there was a change over from tubs to mine cars. The onsetters at that time were Stan Kennedy and W. Peacock.

Above: Murton Colliery after closure. This view shows the pit head baths. In 1910 the Riot Act was read to the Murton miners on the pit heap and 200 police charged the pitmen with many injuries. There was a brickworks at the colliery until 1958. The name on the bricks was 'Milford' – not 'Murton'.

Right: The shaft of Murton Colliery looking over to the A19.

Horden Colliery. Shaft sinking commenced in 1900 with the shaft passing through 425 feet of water bearing limestone. Sinking of the North and South shafts, each 20 feet in diameter, was completed in 1904. The East shaft, 17 feet in diameter, was completed in 1908. Manpower at the colliery was – 1947: 3,926 men; 1954: 3,374 men; 1969: 2,071 men and 1973: 1,820 men. Between 1962 and 1967, reconstruction of the colliery was carried out.

The demolition of Horden Colliery in 1986.

Shotton Colliery. Sunk in 1840, the pit was closed in the 1870s before being re-opened by Horden Collieries Ltd. The pit finally closed in 1972.

Wingate Grange Colliery. Sunk in 1837, the colliery was closed in 1962. This photograph was taken in 1906 at the time of an explosion at the pit when 24 men were killed. The scene shows worried families at the pit waiting for news of their loved ones underground.

Dean and Chapter Colliery, Ferryhill. Sunk in 1902 by the Bolckow & Vaughan mining company, the pit closed in 1966. This pit was the largest in the Ferryhil area and once employed 1,500 men and boys who produced around 450,000 tons of coal a year.

Leasingthorne Colliery. The pit was sunk in 1842 and closed in 1965. At the colliery's peak, 1,000 men and boys were employed, producing around 300,000 tons of coal a year.

Windlestone Colliery. Sunk in 1877 by Pease and Partners, the colliery was 'laid idle' in the 1880s when there was a collapse in the price of coal. Around 1895 the pit re-opened until closing for the final time in 1931.

Forgotten Collieries

In a book such as this it is impossible to feature every colliery in the Durham Coalfield. Here are a few that I would like to mention:

Pit	Sunk	Closed
Black Boy, Coundon Gate	1810	1830
Tees Hetton	1830	1894
Coppy Crooks	1835	1852
Evenwood	1840	1896
Furnace Pit, Shildon	1866	1923
Lady Smith	1920	1948
South Shildon All Saints	1925	1958
South Church Drift	1934	1935
Staindrop Field House	1940	1967

Randolph Colliery, Evenwood. Sunk in 1893 by the North Bitchburn Coal Company, the pit was named after one of the owners. The colliery closed in 1962 but a nearby coke works continued for a number of years.

John Henry Pit, Eldon Colliery. Sunk in 1890, John Henry (also known as old Eldon) was part of Eldon Colliery (sunk in 1829). John Henry closed in 1931.

St Helen's Colliery, Bishop Auckland. The colliery had four shafts: Catherine, Emma, Engine and Tindale. The colliery was owned by Pease & Partners and sunk in 1830. The pit closed in the mid 1920s.

Delight Colliery, Dipton. The colliery was first sunk in the 1840s and closed in 1909. A new Delight Pit was sunk in 1909 and survived to 1940 when it closed with the loss of 850 jobs. In 1935 the colliery belonged to John Bowes & Partners of Milburn House, Newcastle.

Beamish No 2 Pit – also known as Chophill. Sunk in the 1880s, the colliery closed in 1962 and was moved to Beamish Museum.

Haswell Colliery. Sunk in 1831, an explosion at the colliery in 1844 claimed 95 lives. There had been 99 men working in the pit at the time – only 4 men got out alive. Haswell Colliery closed in 1896.

Silksworth Colliery. Lord Londonderry bought the rights to mine coal in the Silksworth area and sinking began on 16th August 1869. The Number One shaft was sunk in 1869 with Number Two shaft sunk four years later. The first coal was drawn from the Hutton Seam on 3rd July 1873 and the following month 19 wagons of coal were sold to the Hetton Coal Company. By 1880, 1,484 tons of coal were drawn per day. The manager of the pit in 1898 was F.S. Panton. The pit was sold in 1920 to Lambton & Hetton Collieries Ltd.

In the 1950s £2.5 million of improvements were made to the colliery with a new washery, lamproom and fitting shops. Electric winders replaced steam ones and the old pit head gear replaced. The production banner was won in 1960-61.

To try to save the pit from closure, a roadway was driven to the South Harvey Seam to work the Ryhope coal where the coal went up to 6-7 feet high. The faces at the Silksworth were said to be only 4 feet 6 inches.

The last shift was worked at Silksworth on 4th November 1971. The pit closed two days later. Fifty men worked on salvage at the colliery and that work ended in July 1972. It was estimated that 97 million tons of coal lay ready to be mined.

The Number One man-riding shaft at Silksworth Colliery.

Ryhope Colliery. On 25th April 1856 active sinking operations were commenced with the sod cutting ceremony performed by Miss Louisa Nicholson of Nicholson House, Sunderland. The North and South shafts were completed together in 1859. The North shaft being the downcast and the South shaft being the upcast. The North shaft was 271 fathoms and four feet deep to the Hutton Seam. The South shaft was 254 fathoms and four feet deep to the Maudlin Seam.

From 1947 to 1966 the NCB spent a total of £1,400,000 on capital expenditure. In 1955-56 a new multi-rope tower winding engine with pneumatic rams both on the surface and underground was installed costing £325,000. In 1959 the pit's output came from seven faces but by 1963 operations in the Harvey were stopped. The colliery was losing 31s 5d per ton of coal in 1965-66 and the only year Ryhope made a profit after 1947 was in 1960. The pit was classed as category B – 'future doubtful'. The NCB Divisional Board said the colliery would have to close in November 1966. Dr Reid, Chairman of the Divisional Board, told lodge officials that the reason Ryhope had to close was because of heavy financial losses. Hopes had been pinned on the south side of the Five Quarter Seam but results there were disappointing. Part of the pit's trouble was that the output per man shift was not good enough. A union representative asked if the men are not to blame who is? The chairman replied: 'Mining conditions.'

An appeal against closure was made but a meeting of the NCB in London felt unable to reverse the decision – the colliery must close. This was the nail in the coffin for the Ryhope people. Many thought this was one back from the NCB for the pit having a strong union – there had been 56 stoppages and go slows.

Ryhope Colliery closed on 26th November 1966 with the loss of 801 jobs.

The demolition of the pit head at Ryhope Colliery.

St Hilda Colliery, South Shields. Sunk in 1810, in its early days the colliery was known as Chapter Main. The pit closed in 1940. Coalmining continued in the town until the closure of Westoe Colliery in 1993.

Wearmouth Colliery's 'D' Shaft which was sunk in 1955 and on completion became the main coal-drawing shaft. From here, coal went into bunkers and then to the washery which is the building on the left of the photograph. The 'A' and 'B' shafts at the pit had been sunk in 1826 by Messrs Thompson, Pemberton & Co. Wearmouth, the last deep coalmine in County Durham, was closed in 1993.

Wearmouth was the most well-know pit in Sunderland, however, there was an almost forgotten colliery in the town – Pallion Pit. This colliery, near what is now Ford Field Road, was sunk around 1767 by Mr Goodchild of Pallion Hall. The shaft was 102 feet deep and was closed in the 1800s.

Lambton D Pit. The pit was sunk around 1830 and worked the Busty, Maudlin and Low Seams. The colliery closed in 1965.

Washington Glebe Colliery. The pit, sunk in 1904, became proud production champions in 1962 then closed ten years later.

Herrington Colliery. The pit was sunk in 1874 and closed in 1985. Herrington's pit heaps were removed in 1996 and a park now stands on the site.

Fishburn Colliery. Sunk in 1910 by H. Stobart, the colliery closed in 1973. In 1954 a £2 million coking plant was built at Fishburn. The cokeworks survived thirteen years after the colliery closed

Fishburn Colliery underground locomotive garage where loco fitter Chris Sargent worked all his life.

Wooley Colliery, Crook. The pit was sunk in 1864 by Pease and Partners. The colliery was closed in 1927, opened up again in 1929, closed in 1931 and opened for a third time in 1937. Wooley Colliery finally closed in 1963.

The engine room at Wooley Colliery. The pit was linked underground to the nearby Roddymoor Colliery where the coals were drawn.

Langley Park Colliery. The pit was sunk by the Consett Iron Company in 1873 and closed in 1975. At the colliery was the Kay Burn Shaft as well as Hutton Drift, Blue Bell Drift and Langley Hall Drift.

Collieries Owned by the Consett Iron Company, 1864-1947

Westwood Colliery	Derwent Colliery	Medomsley Colliery
Billingside Drift	Eden Colliery	Tin Mill Colliery
Delves Colliery	Crookhall Colliery	Ellimore Colliery
Bradley Colliery	Brooms Drift	Iveston Colliery
Humber Hill Drift	Langley Park Colliery	Woodside Winning Drift
Chopwell Colliery	Whittonstall Drift	Garesfield Colliery

On the colliery side, the manpower of the Consett Iron Company rose steadily. In 1892 the collieries employed 2,439 men which had risen to 8,316 men in 1911 and 10,641 men before the 1926 strike. After the strike and the Depression, pit closures cut this number by half by 1946.

Before the First World War, the Consett Iron Company was raising well over 2 million tons of coal a year.

Chopwell Colliery. Number One shaft was sunk in the 1890s. There were a further two shafts at this Consett Iron Company pit. In 1955 the Hutton Drift closed and the East Drift opened in 1956. The coal was worked at Hollins West Drift until the colliery closed in 1966.

Greenwells Wood Drift Mine. It was worked under private ownership by the Lanchester & Iveston Company – and was never under the NCB. This photograph was taken in 1994 after closure of the drift mine.

Middridge Drift Mine. Mining at the drift started in 1954 by the NCB and closed in 1966. It was opened up again by the Young Group as a licensed mine. The men handfilled into tubs. The drift finally closed around 1993 and top soil was put over the drift. The area is now a grass field and you would not know there had been a mine here.

An old drift mine near Frosterley.

MEN AT WORK

Fred Bowe of Medomsley. Fred worked at Medomsley Elm Park Drift Mine before moving on to Marley Hill Colliery and then to Vane Tempest Colliery. Here, Fred is pony putting in the Busty Seam of Marley Hill Colliery in 1975.

George Charlton (left), safety engineer, with a visitor to Vane Tempest Colliery.

Driving a wedge into bottom coal at Brancepeth Colliery.

Above: Miners at work in a Durham pit using a hand ratchet drill. This type of work was very hard with only an oil lamp for illumination underground.

Right: A group of men at Easington Colliery. The darkest day at this pit was on 29th May 1951 when eighty-one miners and two rescue workers were killed following an explosion.

On the surface at Brusselton Colliery, near Shildon. Ted Laskey is on the far right.

Face supports being set up in a Durham pit where the coal was very high.

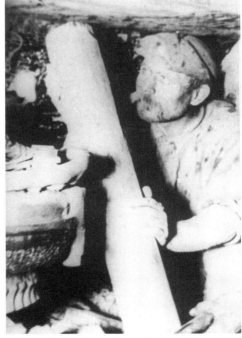

A much earlier view of a miner in a Durham pit with a low face.

Peter Frecker, of Silksworth, at Wearmouth Colliery, looking at an old pump that had been found down the pit.

Miners take a break at the Hole in the Wall Colliery, Crook.

SIGNALS

GUARD/SHUNTER Give clear and distinct signals using one of the following methods:

	HAND LAMP	BELL	WHISTLE
STOP	RED LIGHT	ONE RING	ONE LONG BLAST
PROCEED TOWARDS SIGNALLER	GREEN LIGHT WAVED VERTICALLY	TWO RINGS	TWO SHORT BLASTS
PROCEED AWAY FROM SIGNALLER	GREEN LIGHT WAVED HORIZONTALLY	THREE RINGS	THREE SHORT BLASTS

In an emergency, the signal STOP may be given by other persons.

The front and back of a card giving instructions for the driver and guard/shunter of underground locomotives at Vane Tempest Colliery.

DRIVER   Give audible warning :

1. before moving the locomotive
2. when persons are in front of the locomotive
3. when approaching a curve and at intervals along the curve
4. when approaching and not less than 12 metres/15 yards from any switch, junction or ventilation door.

FIXED LIGHT SIGNALS

RED LIGHT	STOP. WAIT UNTIL SIGNAL CLEARS
GREEN LIGHT	GO
NO INDICATION SHOWING	STOP. ASSUME RED LIGHT

SIDE TWO

A visit to Vane Tempest Colliery. Coming out of the cage, on the right, is Maurice Kirk.

Miners from Silksworth Colliery. Jack Dunne is the foreoverman with the stick. Tom Hays is fifth along and next to him is Bill Richardson.

A pitman hewing coals at Brancepeth Colliery, Willington.

Miners at Croxdale Colliery in the late nineteenth century.

Men coming out of Wearmouth around 1966.

The Certificate of Training of Alan Cook who worked at Silksworth.

Robert Scott Youern (right) with another pitman before a shift at Wearmouth Colliery in the 1940s. Unfortunately, the name of the other miner is not known.

39

COAL MINES ACT, 1911

COAL MINES (TRAINING) GENERAL REGULATIONS, 1945

CERTIFICATE
of Training for Employment at the Coal Face

(Prescribed by the Minister of Fuel and Power in pursuance of Regulation 4 (1) (c) of the above-mentioned Regulations.)

This is to certify that [1] J. Potts
9 Coronation Aven. Fishburn

has been employed for at least [2] (eighty) (one hundred and ten) working days on work below ground in a coal mine, has duly received the training mentioned in sub-paragraph (b) of paragraph (1) of Regulation 4 of the above-mentioned Regulations in the operations specified in the Schedule hereto and is competent to be employed at the coal face.

Date 23-10-54

Signed Geo. B. Deley

Training Officer for the Fishburn Mine

SCHEDULE (3)

1. The getting of coal, including the filling or loading of coal for removal from the coal face.

2. The building of packs or the withdrawal of supports from the waste, or, in a case in which packs are built and supports withdrawn from the waste in the mine in which the person to whom this certificate relates is to be employed, the building of packs and the withdrawal of supports from the waste.

3. The ripping of the roof or floor, including the building of roadside packs in a case in which such packs are built in the mine in which the person to whom this certificate relates is to be employed.

4. The shifting of mechanical conveyors and gate-end loaders.

5. The use of machines for cutting coal or for getting and loading coal.

NOTES: (1) Insert full name and address.

(2) Strike out whichever figure is not required. The number must be at least eighty if training has been given on a face wholly for training purposes and one hundred and ten if given on a face partly reserved for training purposes.

(3) Strike out those operations in which training was not given during the period to which this certificate refers.

Above: Men and boys at the shaft bottom of Brancepeth Colliery, Willington.

Left: The Certificate of Training for Employment at the Coal Face of T. Potts who worked at Fishburn Colliery in the 1950s.

Men at Seaham Colliery. Included are: Chuck Bamburgh, Adam Woods, Jackie Greenwood, Chris Errington, Jimmy Sinnet, Ray Beasdale, Old Sid Strong, John Dobinson, Charlie McCabe, Jimmy Marrin, John Owen, Jerry Carrol, ? Dixon, Jack Thine and Teddy Bailey.

Miners at Dawdon Colliery, Seaham, come up from their shift in the 1970s.

Pony putting at Blackburn Fell Drift Mine, Byermoor.

A putter and driver at Brancepth Colliery in the 1930s.

Tom Turnbull when he was with the Houghton Mines' Rescue. Later, Tom became fire officer at Vane Tempest Colliery and before that he worked as a powerloader at Eppleton Colliery.

H.M. Divisional Inspector of Mines,
Crown Buildings
63 Westgate Road
Newcastle upon Tyne.

Date as Postmark

Dear Sir,

I am pleased to forward herewith your Certificate of Qualification as a Deputy/Shotfirer.

You will observe that the Certificate has provision made for the record of Gas Testing Certificates and renewals obtained by you. On your appointment you will be required to submit the Gas Testing Certificate to the Manager of the mine who will then make the necessary entries on your Certificate.

Kindly acknowledge receipt on the enclosed "Official Paid" postcard and return it to me at your earliest convenience.

Yours faithfully,

WALTER WIDDAS

H.M. Divisional Inspector of Mines and Quarries.

A Certificate of Qualification for a deputy.

QUICK THINKING DATAL HAND

A Power Loader was trapped under a large stone at the tail gate end of the C33 Unit.

An Airborne Dust Sampler, Shaun Ryan, was in the vicinity and heard the shouts of the Power Loader.

Shaun receiving his Miner's Lamp from Mr. I. Smith.

He immediately without hesitation went into the area and played a vital role in freeing the trapped man.

At a recent Consultative Meeting Shaun was presented with a Miner's Lamp, by Mr. I Smith, the Colliery Manager in recognition of his swift action.

Above: The Fire and Rescue Team at Crook. The Coal Mines' Act of 1911 made it the duty of coal owners to establish central rescue stations within a ten mile radius of collieries. The rescue station building at Crook still stands today but is used by pigeon fanciers to store their equipment.

Left: A cutting from a colliery newsletter from 1989. It shows Shaun Ryan, of Vane Tempest Colliery, receiving a miners' lamp after freeing a power loader who was trapped under a large stone.

COLLIERY COMMUNITIES

Miners' housing in the 1920s. These houses would have had an outside toilet and one water tap for the whole street.

Left: The back lane of Brick Row, Ryhope. Note the 'stable' double doors which allow the 'bottom' to be closed while this housewife looks out of the open 'top' door.

Above: A soup kitchen set up during hard times in Ryhope. These soup kitchens were essential during a strike when food was scarce and any resources were shared amongst the colliery community.

Right: Robert Scott Youern with his wife Elsie, daughter Elsie and son Arthur in the backyard of No 7 Brooke Street, Sunderland. They lived in the area known as 'Back of the Pit' – near Wearmouth Colliery. Robert was a pitman at Wearmouth.

William Houghton, Amy Guest, Doreen Delaney and Arthur Youern in
Richmond Street, Sunderland.

James Owens, Arthur Youern and David Templeton outside the Road
Weighbridge at Wearmouth Colliery in 1991.

The pit pony, Lion, from Harraton Colliery who won numerous prizes at shows all over the country. A well-known pony-owning family in County Durham were William and Fred Laws of Willington who traded with the private coal owners and the NCB from 1915 to 1964. In 1915 a pony cost around £15 10s while in 1963 the price was £44. In 1947 the Law family supplied 905 ponies to the NCB. In 1963 the last 11 sales were made by the Laws.

Right: The County show at Westerhope in 1949. Matty the pit pony from Ellemore Colliery won the first prize.

Above: A night out at Silksworth Hall, 5th November 1971. The night had been organised by the union as the pit was due to close the following day and was the last gathering of local miners.
Included are: Peter Foster, Pat Quinn, Gary Cooper, Natie Quinn, Ube McCabe and Dick Mugridge.

Left: Sixteen-year-old John Spanton outside the colliery offices at Ryhope in 1915. John worked at Ryhope from 1912 to 1963.

A postcard of the Durham Miners' Hall at Red Hills, opened 23rd October 1915.

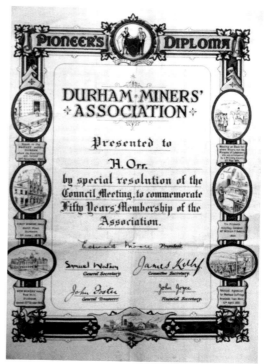

The union card for F. Jackson, NUM Durham Area, Eppleton Lodge. Each week a man paid his union dues which were written down on his card.

Mr H. Orr's fifty years membership of the Durham Miners' Association. Mr Orr worked at Silksworth Colliery.

Ulverston, Conishead Priory

Conishead Priory Convalescent Home in Ulverston could accommodate 120 guests at a time. A brochure produced in the 1950s called *Facilities For Better Health in the Durham Coalfield* described the convalescent home:

'The Home, which has extensive grounds covering 220 acres, lies at the southern end of the Lake District on the shores of Morecambe Bay. Patients are transported by special motor coach which leaves Durham on alternative Fridays.

Managed by a committee representative of the National Coal Board and the Durham County Mining Federation Board, the Home is supervised by a Superintendent and a Matron (a State Registered Nurse).

Darts, dominoes and a television room provide indoor entertainment, while outside there are facilities for bowls and putting. There are, too, organised outings to the Lakes, Blackpool and to football matches during the season.

Guests are accepted throughout the year, except in December and the first fortnight in January when the Home is closed for cleaning and decoration.

Approaching 70,000 have attended the Home since it was opened in 1930.'

The Home closed in 1969 and is now a Buddhist Centre.

In 1949 Londonderry Collieries gave the Durham Miners' Association a building and grounds in Tempest Road, Seaham, to be converted into a clinic. It was named the Londonderry Dene House Miners' Rheumatic Clinic and treated out-patients with rheumatic conditions.

The Hermitage – Durham Miners' Rehabilitation Centre, Chester-le-Street

The Hermitage was opened in 1944 by the Miners' Welfare Commission for injured Durham men. The centre was transferred to the NHS in 1956 and injured workers who were not miners were admitted. The 1950s brochure described the regime at The Hermitage:

'After periods in hospital, mineworkers and other injured patients are referred to the Centre for intensive rehabilitation to restore their physical fitness. The treatment is an active one of remedial exercises, swimming, games, work preparation and conditioning. This operates Mondays to Fridays from 8.45 am until 4.15 pm. The patients return home to spend the weekend with their families.

Each year about 400 miner patients and others receive treatment for an average period of eight weeks.'

The Sam Watson Rest Home in Richmond. This description of the home was given in the 1950s:

'First priority is the wives of NCB employees and female NCB employees in the Durham Coalfield. Consideration can also be given to applications from the wives of redundant miners who have not taken up employment outside the mining industry, the widows of deceased workmen and in exceptional cases, justified on medical grounds, applications for a second stay at the Home.

The Home is one where the tired or not-so-well mother can stay a fortnight and return to her household duties re-invigorated by the rest, good food, cheerful company and tonic North Yorkshire fresh air.

It has all the best features of a first-class holiday hotel, without fuss and regimentation. Obviously, there must be some rules, but they have been kept to a minimum and are designed to ensure the smooth running of the establishment and to promote rest and the happiness of the guests.

There are no restrictions on movement. Guests can come and go as they please, having regard of course to meal times.'

A group at the Sam Watson Rest Home in 1995. Doris Gillum (née Cahill) is second from the left, second row from the front. Her husband, Fred, worked at Ryhope Colliery. Doris' sister-in-law, also called Doris, is front, far right. Her husband, John 'Doc' Gillum, worked at Silksworth. The matron at that time was Mrs Hopper.

Left: The banner of the Durham Aged Mineworkers' Homes Association. The DAMHA was founded in 1898 by Joseph Hopper from Sheriff Hill, Gateshead. He was a lay preacher, and well-known for his speaking skills, who launched the idea of providing homes for aged miners at a meeting in 1894. Four years later the DAMHA was established with John Wilson MP as its chairman. Wilson worked at a number of collieries and for 33 years was the agent for the Durham Miners' Association. He also served as the Mid-Durham MP.

This banner was first displayed at the 100th Durham Miners' Gala in 1983. The front shows John Wilson MP and Joseph Hopper, with the Castlereagh Homes on Seaham Harbour seafront.

A Souvenir to Commemorate

60th ANNIVERSARY
of the opening of

JOSEPH HOPPER MEMORIAL HOMES
WINDY NOOK

A Commemorative Service will be held on
Thursday 29th November 1984 at 2.30p.m. in
WINDY NOOK METHODIST CHURCH

Followed by a procession to the
JOSEPH HOPPER MEMORIAL HOMES
where afternoon tea and light refreshments will be
served for the residents of the homes and guests of
Durham Aged Mineworkers' Homes Association.

Right: The cover of a souvenir booklet to commemorate the 60th anniversary of the opening of the Joseph Hopper Memorial Homes, Windy Nook, Gateshead. A commemorative service was held on 29th November 1984 at Windy Nook Methodist Church.

The DAMHA is still going strong today under its director, John Humble. John comes from a long line of miners – his father started at North Biddick Colliery and was later transferred to Harraton before finishing off as fore-overman at Seaham Colliery.

Browney Colliery Band in the 1930s.

Silksworth Colliery Band outside the Welfare Hall in Silksworth.

THE DURHAM MINERS' GALA

The Hetton Lodge Banner at the 1929 Gala.

The Miners' Gala started in 1871, two years after the formation of the Durham Miners' Association. The first Gala was at Wharton Park in Durham City. After Nationalisation in 1947 there were 127 pits in Durham, although not all were fully represented at the Gala as some lodges did not have a banner – they did not have the money to buy one! Small Lodges such as Metal Bridge and Stanley Cottages Lodges never had banners.

In 1969 it was the centenary of the formation of the Durham Miners' Association and 25 banners of collieries that had closed were marched through the streets of Durham. That Gala was also a sad day as two miners had been killed the night before at Easington Colliery. Fourteen men were saved as they scrambled clear of a fall of stone.

The 1986 Gala saw an estimated 10,000 people turn out. One of the main attractions that day was over 100 banners displayed in a marque on the Gala field. Among the collection was the Tursdale Banner of 1893.

The peak of the mining industry in Durham was in 1913 when 164,246 men were employed, producing 40 million tons of coal per year.

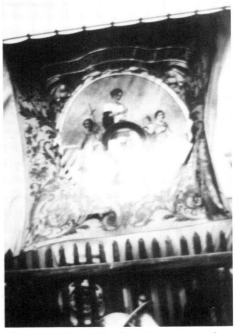

The Burnhope Lodge Banner at the Gala in the 1940s. The pit was sunk in 1845 and closed in 1949.

Two views of the West Auckland Lodge Banner at the Gala in the early 1960s.
A.J. Horner (NUM General Secretary and who appears on the banner) is with
lodge members and their families in the above photograph.

The Ryhope Banner coming out of Durham in 1965. This was the last time this banner was at the Gala while the colliery was working. The pit was closed the following year.

The Ryhope Lodge Banner at the Gala in the 1960s.

The Silksworth Lodge Banner at the Gala. Bill Boarder, who was union man at Silksworth Colliery, is sitting with his family. This banner went back to Ryhope Lodge in the 1980s.

The Brussleton Lodge Banner at the Gala in the 1960s. Reg Hindmarsh, lodge official, is second left.

The Seaham Lodge Banner at the Gala in 1972. On the left side, carrying the banner, is Jack Robinson. At the front of the banner is Jack Burns, Fred Clenell and Steve Johnson. All of these men worked at Silksworth Colliery before being transferred to Seaham in 1971.

One of the bands has a rest in the city centre at a Gala in the 1980s.

Everyone pauses below the balcony of the County Hotel in the 1980s.

Below the balcony of the County Hotel – a focal point for every Gala.

A packed scene around the County Hotel in the 1980s.

The morning of the Gala in the 1980s.

Waiting for the banners – on the balcony is Arthur Scargill.

Above: Families march in front of the Horden Lodge Banner at the centenary Gala in 1983.

Left: Sacriston Lodge Banner at the centenary Gala in 1983.

Above: Shotton
Lodge Banner at
the 1983 Gala.

Right: Eden
Lodge Banner at
the Gala in
1983.

The Silksworth Lodge Banner at the Gala in 1987. The following were lads
from Silksworth Colliery, left to right: Peter Shields (fitter), Aidan Robins
(overman), Derek Gillum (datal and powerloader), Kevin O'Conner and
Stephen Thompson.

The Durham Union
Banner coming
down from Red Hills
on the morning of
the Gala.

The Vane Tempest Banner at the Gala with the production banner. At the front of the banner are: Bob Hodgson, Brian Frankland and Arthur Oxley – all union men.

The Eldon Lodge Banner. The colliery was sunk in 1829 and closed in 1931. There were three shafts at the pit – John Henry, Harvey and Harry.

The Sacriston Lodge Banner going on to the Gala field in 1994.

The Byers Green Lodge Banner at the 1994 Gala.

The Herrington Lodge Banner at the 1994 Gala.

The Murton Lodge Banner at the 1994 Gala. Two miners and four canteen women carried the Murton Lodge Banner into the Miners' Gala in 1957.

The Chilton Lodge Banner played in by North Skelton Pipe Band at the 1994 Gala.

The Thrislington Lodge Banner going on to the Gala field in 1994.

The Durham Aged Miners' Association Banner at the 1994 Gala.

The Silksworth Lodge Banner at the 1995 Gala.

Above: David Gillum with the Vane Tempest Lodge Banner going into Durham in 1995.

Left: David Gillum with the Ryhope Lodge Banner.

The Vane Tempest Lodge Banner coming into Durham in 1995. Union man, Malcom Smith of Ryhope, is next to the pole.

Two happy lads waiting for the Gala to start at 9 o'clock in 1995. They are George Hutchinson and Keith from Binchester. They both worked at Vane Tempest Colliery.

The
Easington
Lodge
Banner led
by band
master, Mr
Peacock.

The
Herrington
Lodge
Banner
being
played into
the Gala by
a pipe
band.

The Murton Lodge Banner on the Gala field in 1997. Two girls from Silksworth have a chat.

The Browney Lodge Banner at the Gala in 2003. It was made by the Browney Banner Group led by John Kitching and committee.

The Fishburn Lodge Banner at the Gala in 2002.

The Brandon Lodge Banner. Brandon Pit House was sunk in 1924 and closed in 1968.

The South Hetton Lodge Banner at the Gala in 1997. The colliery was sunk in 1831 by the South Hetton Coal Company. The pit was closed in 1983.

Durham Miners' Gala, 9th July 2005
The 121st Big Meeting

The day of the Gala in 2005 was bright and sunny. The first banner on display was the Durham Union Area Banner at 8.40 am. This was followed by the South Hetton Lodge and then the Bevin Boys' Banner. The Gala was now well underway with the bands playing under the balcony of the County Hotel for the VIPs. There was around 70,000 people in Durham that day with 37 bands and 70 banners – more banners than there was in 1960! New banners making their debut at the Gala were Ryhope, Lumley 6th Pit and the Durham Colliery Mechanics' Banner. One of the last banners to make its way on to the Racecourse was the Greenside Lodge at 12.50 pm. This made the speeches 45 minutes late!

The Gala field was packed – just like the old days. It was a red-hot day enjoyed by a large crowd with many bands and banners. At 2.15 pm the banners and bands started to make their way home. The bands started playing *Is This the Way to Amarillo* to the crowds on the banksides leaving the Racecourse. By 4.30 pm the Vane Tempest Lodge Banner got into the Market Square. A few years ago all the banners would have been away by 3.30.

They may have closed our pits but they cannot kill the spirit of our Gala.

In the Market Place at 9.30 am. George Rowe is with the Lambton Banner.

The Fire Brigades Banner in a packed Market Square.

The Shotton Lodge Banner is led through the streets of Durham.

The VIPs on the balcony of the County Hotel.

The new Ryhope Lodge Banner, made in 2005. They were played in by the Wansbeck Ashington Colliery Band.

Lads and lasses with the Vane Tempest Lodge Banner.

The Elemore Lodge Banner on the Gala field.

Two happy folk with the Browney Lodge Banner.

A busy Gala field with the lodge banners resting on the fence.

Above: On the Gala field. Left to right, the lodge banners of: Lumley, Chopwell, East Hetton and Trimdon.

Right: Lumley 6th Pit Lodge Banner, made in 2005. Funds for the banner were raised by John Parkin and the Lion & the Lamb Banner Group.

Above: The Wingate Banner with Fat Al's Band outside the County Hotel on Big Meeting Day, 9th July 2005.

Left: An advert for the 121st Durham Miners' Gala. The speakers that day were: Dennis Skinner MP, Rodney Bickerstaffe, President of War on Want, Bill Hayes CWU General Secretary and Debbie Coulter, GMB Deputy General Secretary

PIT BANNERS

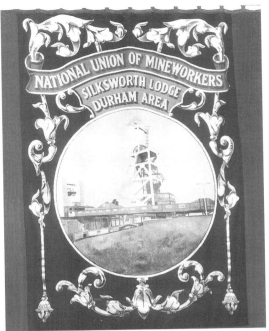
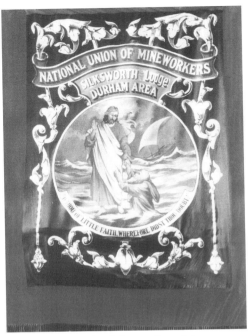
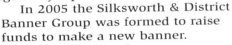

Above: Silksworth Lodge Banner. This banner was acquired from Lambton Lodge after its pit closure around 1965. One side shows Christ walking on water. The other side was painted over and Silksworth Colliery pithead gear replaced the original image. The Lodge also acquired a Ryhope Lodge Banner and this was later transferred to Eppleton Lodge in 1973. This banner was later given back to Ryhope Lodge and it now hangs in Ryhope Workmen's Club.

In 2005 the Silksworth & District Banner Group was formed to raise funds to make a new banner.

Silksworth has also a strong mining society which has been exhibiting mining memoriabilia around County Durham for over five years.

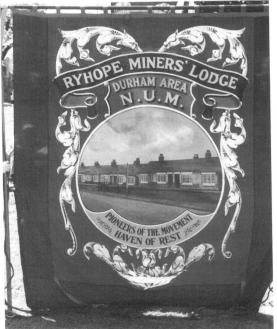

Left: Ryhope Lodge Banner. This banner, made in 1964, shows on one side the Aged Miners' Homes with Conishead Priory on the other. A new banner was made in 2004 by the Ryhope Banner Group. The founders of the group are Malcome Smith and Bob Stephenson, both Ryhope men. Malcome is a former miner and Lodge Official at Vane Tempest Colliery in Seaham.

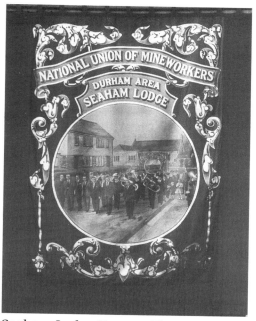

Horden Banner. The banner, made in the 1950s, shows 'Peace and Goodwill to all Miners'.

Seaham Lodge Banner. The reverse of this banner shows 'Suffer Little Children to Come unto Me.'

Right: Harraton Lodge Banner. The colliery was sunk in the 1750s and closed in 1965. The lodge closed the following year. The banner shows 'Friendship, Love and Truth'. A new Harraton Lodge Banner was paraded at the 2004 Gala.

Hylton Lodge Banner. This side shows Keir Hardy while the reverse shows 'Friendship, Love and Truth'. In the 1960s this banner was replaced with one with a view of Hylton Castle with the slogan 'Unity is Strength'. The other side of this banner showed the Aged Miners' Homes.

New Herrington Lodge Banner. This banner, from around the 1930s, shows 'Emancipation of Labour' while the reverse side has Conishead Priory.

Above and right:
Two views of
Houghton Lodge
Banner. The
colliery, sunk in
1827, was
production
champions in 1967
and 1971. The pit
closed on 26th
September 1981.

Follonsby Lodge (Wardley) Banner. Three well known men appear on this banner. Kier Hardie was speaker at the Durham Miners' Gala in 1905, 1906 and 1910. He was a Lanarkshire miner at the age of ten before becoming Secretary of the Ayrshire Miners and the first Labour Member of Parliament. He appears on a number of Lodge Banners, including: Hylton, Heworth and Chilton. Also on the Follonsby Banner are Anthony Joyce and E. Justice.

Springwell Lodge Banner. Springwell Colliery was sunk in 1824 by Lord Ravensworth and Partners and closed in 1931. A banner was made for the Lodge in 1873. The banner in this photograph, made in 2001, was funded by the group started by Derek Scott and his fellow committee members from Springwell. Derek had been a training officer at Westoe Colliery.

Lumley Sixth Pit Lodge Banner. The colliery, once owned by Lord Joicey, was closed in 1966.

Kimblesworth Lodge Banner. The colliery, near Chester-le-Street, was sunk in 1873 and closed in 1967. The Lodge was a member of the DMA from 1878.

Sacriston Lodge Banner. This banner of 1919, shows J. Wilson seated and W. House standing. The reverse shows a hospital ward at the time of the First World War.

Sacriston Lodge Banner. The pit was sunk in 1839 and was linked to Witton Colliery. This banner was produced by the banner makers, Tutill, in 1957.

Witton Lodge Banner. The colliery was sunk in 1859/60. It shows three men of merit: T.H. Cann, J. Wilson and J. Lawson.

Esh Winning Lodge. The banner shows the Miners' Hall in Durham. However, the village of Esh Winning was famous for its own magnificent miners' hall which had a concert hall, cinema, swimming baths, billiard room, games room and library.

Waterhouses Lodge Banner. The colliery was sunk between 1856 and 1857 by the mine owner Joseph Pease. The banner has on it the portraits of three DMA officials:
J. Johnson, J. Wilson and W. House.

Above: Page Bank Banner. After the closure of Page Bank Lodge, the banner was transferred to the nearby Whitworth Park Lodge.

Left: Mainsforth Lodge Banner. The banner was made in 1951. This side shows Conishead Priory Convalescent Home while the other side has an illustration of 'Peace and Haven'.

Tudhoe Lodge Banner. This banner was transferred from Ouston E Lodge. There were many collieries in the Tudhoe area. They included: Tudhoe Colliery, Tudhoe Mill, Tudhoe Park Drift and Tudhoe Grange Colliery.

Dean and Chapter Lodge Banner. This banner, first unfurled in Ferryhill Market Place in 1955, shows Durham Cathedral on one side and different races of the world in friendship on the other.

Whitworth Park Lodge Banner. This banner originally belonged to the New Shildon Lodge and was acquired by Whitworth Park Lodge in the 1960s.

Two views of the Adventure Lodge Banner. The colliery was first sunk in 1815 by Lord Londonderry. It was sold to the Cooks family from the west of Durham in 1912 and they sunk a drift around that time. The drift became the property of the NCB after nationalisation and closed in 1978.

Handon Hold Lodge Banner. This banner was used by the Handon Hold Lodge until 1968 and then was passed on to the Murton Lodge.

Thornley Lodge Banner. The pit was sunk in 1834/35 by Gully & Partners to work the Harvey Seam. When the pit closed in 1970 there were 800 men working there – 160 transferred to Easington Colliery and about 85 men went to Vane Tempest and Seaham Collieries. The rest were distributed among pits including: Shotton, Easington, Fishburn, Blackhall, Hordon, Eppleton, Dawdon, Metal Bridge, Murton, Elemore and South Hetton. Three hundred men were made redundant.

Thrislington Lodge Banner. This banner was produced by the Tutill works in the 1930s. Coal had been mined in this area as early as 1329 but the first deep pit was sunk in 1835. This pit, known as West Cornforth Colliery, closed in 1857. A second colliery was sunk in 1867 and was known as Thrislington Colliery which closed in 1967.

Byermoor Lodge Banner. The pit was sunk in the 1770s and by 1968, when the pit closed, there were 150 Lodge members. This banner was transferred to Vane Tempest Lodge.

South Moor Banner No 1 Lodge – Louisa Old Colliery. This banner was acquired from St Hilda Colliery in South Shields. Notice the pier on the banner – there is no pier or sea at Stanley!

Crook Drift Lodge Banner – the Hole in the Wall Pit. The main part of the colliery was on the Church bank at Crook. The mine had many drifts linked to the main part of the pit. The old part of the colliery –Hole in the Wall – was sunk in 1843. The new Hole in the Wall Colliery was sunk in 1936 and closed in 1964.

Rough Lea Lodge Banner. This banner was found in a hall in Willington by builders. It is now at Red Hills, the Durham Union Area Offices.

Black Prince Lodge Banner. The colliery was sunk on the Tow Law Fell by the Weardale Iron and Coal Company in 1845. The banner, made by Tutill, was transferred to the Hedley Hope Lodge.

Two views of Eldon Drift Banner. The drift was sunk in 1934 and closed in 1962.

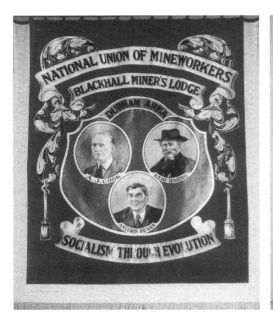
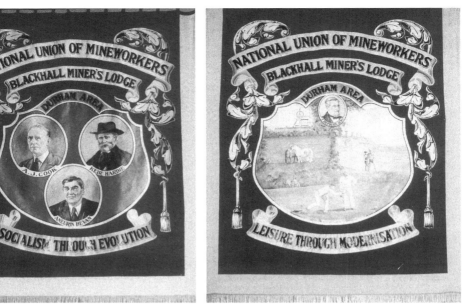

Two views of Blackhall Lodge Banner. Sunk in the early 1900s, the colliery closed in 1981.

Usher Moor Lodge Banner. The front of the banner shows Jack Joyce while the reverse is a view of Red Hills. Usher Moor Colliery was closed in 1960.

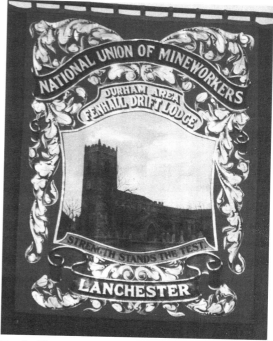

Shotton Lodge Banner. The banner, like many in the Durham coalfield, shows Conishead Priory Convalescent Home.

Fenhall Drift Lodge Banner. This drift mine near Lanchester was sunk in 1954 and closed in 1963.

Greenside Lodge Banner. Greenside Colliery was sunk in 1902 by the Stella Coal Company. The pit closed in 1966.

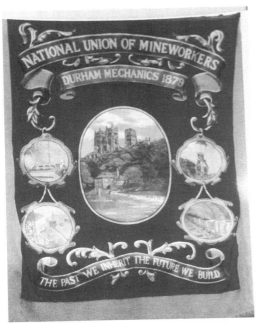

Durham Mechanics Banner. This is the banner of the Mechanics' Union which was started in 1879.

Horden Mechanics Banner. This banner was produced during the Miners' Strike of 1984/85.

NACODS Lodge Banner. The banner of the National Association of Colliery Overmen, Deputies and Shotfirers was first unfurled in 1963.

Durham Cokemen's Banner. This banner, representing seven cokeworks, had originally belonged to the Silksworth Lodge and was made by Tutill in 1938. The banner features portraits of Keir Hardy, A.J. Cook and Peter Lee.

Notable Men

Several lodge banners contain the portraits of the men who shaped the mining industry and the union over the years.

Peter Lee (who appears on the Cokemen's banner) was born in Trimdon Grange and had worked in 16 collieries by the age of 22. In 1902 he was made check weighman by the miners of Wheatley Hill. The following year he was elected to the Parish Council and later became Chairman. Peter Lee had a major impact in the area around Wheatley Hill – establishing the cemetery, sewage system and street lighting in the village and improved local roads. He later became Chairman of Durham County Council after Labour became the ruling party in 1919. In the 1930s he was the General Secretary of the Durham Miners' Association. He died in 1935.

A.J. Cook (who appears on the Eldon Drift Lodge Banner) was the miners' leader during the 1926 strike. During the conflict he addressed a mass meeting at Burnhope.

John Wilson (who appears on the Waterhouses Lodge Banner) started work at Ludworth Colliery at the age of thirteen. He soon became a union representative and eventually lost his job at Wheatley Hill Colliery during a pay dispute. In 1882 he was elected treasurer of the DMA and became MP for Houghton-le-Spring three years later.

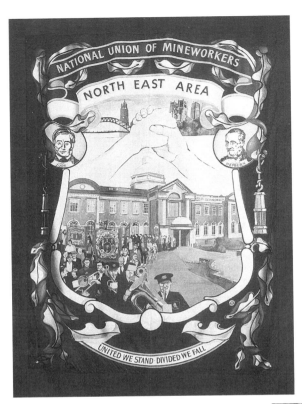

The North East Area Banner. This was made in 1991 by John Midgley of Chippenham Design.

The Bevin Boys Association Banner. The Bevin Boys were called up for National Service during the Second World War. During the war, 33 ballots were held at fortnightly intervals and 20,896 men were selected to work in the pits. There were a further 4,164 who volunteered to work in the mines and 15,657 'optants' who opted for employment in the coal industry in lieu of service in the armed forces. Former service personnel totalled 6,651 and there were 41 conscientious objectors who worked down the pits.

PRESERVING OUR HERITAGE

West Stanley Disaster Memorial. There was an explosion at West Stanley Colliery (the Burns Pit) on 16th February 1909 at 3.45 pm. The explosion had gone its full course ripping through the seams and galleries. In the Townley Seam, at 123 fathoms, 63 men and boys lay dead. The Tilley Seam, 10 fathoms lower, claimed 18. In the Busty Seam the victims numbered 38. The deepest seam worked lay at 163 fathoms and there 48 men and boys were killed. Of those who lost their lives that day, 60 were under the 20 years of age. Fourteen year old Jimmy Gardner died before the remaining men could be led to safety.

The West Stanley Disaster Fund was set up soon afterwards. Miners from Axwell Park Colliery donated a shilling a man from their wages. Stargate and Clara Vale Collieries followed suit. Bill Gardner, one of the 26 men rescued from the Tilley Seam, went around the town with his pony, Paddy, pulling an empty tub. Paddy was one of the 17 ponies found alive. People were invited to throw their contributions into the tub.

A total of 168 men and boys died in the explosion at West Stanley Colliery – the most number of men ever killed in a disaster in a Durham pit.

The

50th

Anniversary of
Easington Colliery Pit Disaster

29th May 1951

Opening of the Community Memorial Garden

Memorial Service and Dedication

Left: The cover of a commemorative booklet to mark the opening of the community garden in memory of the 50th anniversary of the Easington Colliery disaster.

The cover of the booklet for the ninety-fifth Miners' Festival Service, 10th July 2004. At the service the Bishop of Durham, the Right Reverend Dr Tom Wright, dedicated the following new lodge banners: Wingate, Harraton, Easington, Browney, Lambton, Houghton and Coxhoe. The banners were dedicated as 'a symbol of the fellowship and service of our local people.'

The Cathedral Church of Christ and Blessed Mary the Virgin Durham

The Ninety-Fifth

Miners' Festival Service

Saturday 10 July 2004
3.00 p.m.

NUM (North East Area) Band
Music Director: Mr Barry Holden
with the NUM Area Banner and the Wingate and Harraton banners

Easington Colliery Band
Music Director: Stuart Gray
with the Easington Banner

Esh & Bearpark Colliery Band
Bandmaster: Michael Evans
with the Browney Colliery Miners' Lodge Banner

Lynthwaite Silver Band
Music Director: Steve Platten
with the Lambton and Houghton Lodge Banners

Langbargh Band
Music Director: Tim Oldroyd
with the Coxhoe Bridge Drift Banner

Tom Pickard from Easington with pony and tub on 29th May 2001.

An exhibition of mining memorabilia and photographs at Tudhoe Village in the summer of 2003. Derek Gillum is with his wife, Jean, and Mrs Eileen Bowbanks.

Delves Lane Village Hall

Delves Lane Village Hall is an ex-miners' Welfare Hall built in 1925. The upkeep at that time was paid for by deductions from the miners' wages. In 1979 the National Coal Board handed over the building to the residents and Delves Lane Community Association was formed. Sadly, following the closure of the coalmines in the area the usage and interest in the building gradually faded. The building became outdated and a roundabout saga unfolded – uninviting premises failed to encourage people to use them and so running costs were difficult to find.

In 1997 a regeneration programme was introduced and fundraising events arranged to pay for a part-time cleaner in an attempt to encourage usage and raise awareness of the village hall once again. Funding was found to provide equipment for new activities and slowly the tide began to turn. With the approach of the new millennium more money became available and £800,000 was secured to allow total refurbishment and extension with disabled friendliness. New facilities include an outdoor play area and all-weather multi-surface sports pitch.

In 1999 the premises were temporarily closed down to allow refurbishment to be completed. In December of that year HRH Princess Ann chose Delves Lane Village Hall as being an outstanding community achievement and on 11th February 2000 HRH officially re-opened the premises spending a morning with local people – something they will never forget.

The village hall has once again become the heart of the community.

An illustration of coal filling by former pitman, Ron Gray. Ron published a collection of his illustrations, poems and short stories in his book *Kist Crack*. The 'Kist' – Norwegian for box – was where deputies and shot firers would meet.

COAL FILLER Ron Gray '05

'MARRAS'
Ron Gray 05'

Another Ron Gray illustration of a pony and putter, Ron says: 'Quite often during bait time, a putter would catch forty winks. One story I heard was of a putter falling asleep and when he awoke his pony had eaten most of his bait. Most putters treat their ponies well and often took their bairns to visit them when the ponies were put out to rest during the summer holidays. The putters would also take fresh hay or sweets during the shift.'

A rally was held at Thornley in 2005 when eleven banners marched from the Crossways Hotel to the village community centre. The occasion was to mark the opening of the Durham Mining Museum. The banners were from: Thornley, Wheatley Hill, Fishburn, Houghton, Elemore, South Hetton, Easington, Horden, Blackhall, Wingate and Murton.

The people of Thornley support their Lodge Banner.

The Thornley Lodge Banner leads the way in the parade.

This banner is a reproduction of the Thornley Lodge Banner of 1872. This new banner was made in 2003.

Wingate Banner and local people at the launch of Thornley Pit Museum, 2nd July 2005. John Cairns, behind the two young girls, is committee member for the Wingate Banner Group.

George Rowe and Pat Simmons with local schoolchildren and the Houghton and Lambton Lodge Banners. George started the Houghton and Lambton Banner Group in 2002 with Pat Simmons and committee. George, who had a serious illness, continued to put the Banner Group first, with Pat backing him all the way. They had fund raising nights at local clubs and sold raffle tickets. The Vardy Group donated £5,000 towards the fund. After a long struggle and lots of hard work they reached their target and the Houghton and Lambton Banners were made and paraded at the Gala in 2004 – a proud day for George and Pat and the local community. The Banner Group continues their work with an education plan in mining history for schools in the area. More banner groups are setting up following the success of the Houghton and Banner Group – a further tribute to the work of George and Pat.

Left: The Lambton Lodge Banner.

A statue of a pitman lifting a tub at Red Hills, the home of the Durham Miners since 1915.

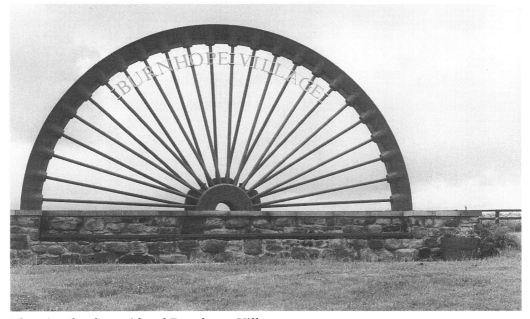

The pit wheel outside of Burnhope Village.

THE PEOPLE'S HISTORY

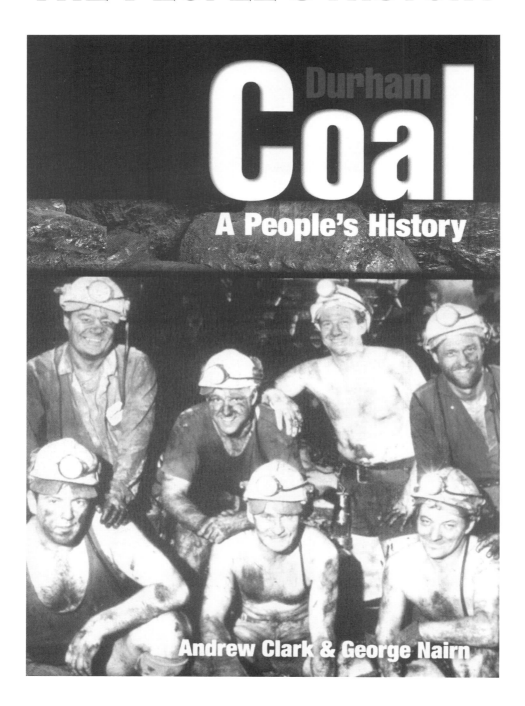

Durham
Coal
A People's History

Andrew Clark & George Nairn

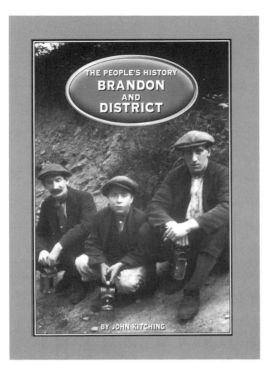

THE PEOPLE'S HISTORY
BRANDON
AND
DISTRICT

BY JOHN KITCHING

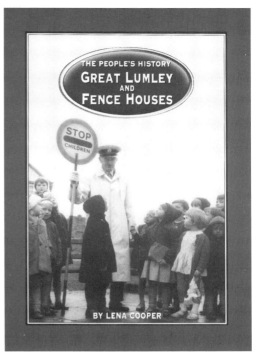

THE PEOPLE'S HISTORY
GREAT LUMLEY
AND
FENCE HOUSES

STOP
CHILDREN

BY LENA COOPER

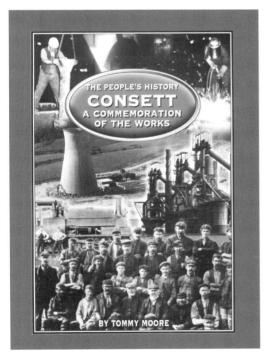

THE PEOPLE'S HISTORY
CONSETT
A COMMEMORATION
OF THE WORKS

BY TOMMY MOORE

THE PEOPLE'S HISTORY
A NOSTALGIC LOOK AT
CONSETT

STOP
CHILDREN
CROSS HER

BY THE DERWENTDALE LOCAL HISTORY SOCIETY

Brancepeth Colliery, Willington. The pit was sunk in 1840 and closed in 1967. After closure, the Park Drift Mine was opened by the Rackwood Coal Company from Yorkshire.

The People's History

To receive a catalogue of our latest titles please send a
large stamped addressed envelope to:

The People's History Ltd
Suite 1
Byron House
Seaham Grange Business Park
Seaham
County Durham
SR7 0PY